The #1 Interview Playbook

A CLEVER GUIDE TO WINNING YOUR FIRST JOB

BOOST YOUR CONFIDENCE & MASTER THE INTERVIEW

A Clever Guide To Winning The Job Interview

Contents Page

Contents Page	Page 2
Disclaimer	Page 6
Acknowledgements	Page 7
About the Author	Page 10
Introduction	Page 11
What to Expect	Page 15
3 Stages To The Interview	Page 17
Different Types of Job Interviews	Page 18
Assessment Centres	Page 18
Informal Interviews	Page 19
Formal Interviews	Page 20
Phone Interviews	Page 21
Virtual Job Interviews	Page 23
Tips For A Virtual Interview	Page 24
Group Interviews	Page 25
One on One Interviews	Page 26
Panel Interviews	Page 27
Potential Interviews From Job Searching	Page 30
Booking the Interview	Page 31
A Professional Voicemail & Email Address	Page 33

Contents Page

Multiple Interview Invitations	Page 34
Research the Company & Industry	Page 35
Research the Interviewer	Page 37
Do You Know The Interview Process?	Page 40
Do You Know Your Resume Inside Out?	Page 41
Do You Want To Get Over Your Nerves & Feel More Confident?	Page 43
How To Avoid These Common Interview Mistakes	Page 48
Interview Guidelines	Page 51
Are You Prepared For The Interview	Page 55
Personal & Professional Social Media Profiles	Page 57
The Law of Reciprocity	Page 58
Control The Conversation	Page 59
Verbal Communication - Be Careful What You Say & How You Say It	Page 61
How Much Should You Share During The Interview?	Page 63
Practice Makes Permanent Not Perfect	Page 65
Use the Interviewers Name	Page 66
How To Answer Challenging Behavioural	Page 67
STAR Method Example	Page 68
What Is Emotional Intelligence?	Page 69

A Clever Guide To Winning The Job Interview

Do You Know How To Mirror and Match to Build Rapport?	Page 71
Use Mirror and Matching to help Build Rapport with the Interviewer	Page 72
Examples of Nonverbal Communication Skills	Page 75
How to Ensure Interview Success?	Page 78
Attitude is Everything	Page 83
Action Verb	Page 85
Action Verb Examples	Page 86
Commonly Asked Interview Questions - Worksheets	Page 91
Additional Interview Questions You Might Be Asked	Page 126
Prepare Your Own Quality Questions	Page 148
Examples Of Quality Questions To Ask The Interviewer	Page 150
First Impressions Count	Page 152
Should You Ask About Pay?	Page 153
Closing Out the Interviewer - Scarcity & Urgency	Page 155
Interview Hints & Tips	Page 157
Self-Assessment Framework	Page 162
Should I Say Yes To Accepting The Job Offer	Page 165
Good Luck	Page 166
Social Media Handles	Page 167
Copyright & Job Search Qld Logo	Page 169

Disclaimer

All the information, techniques, skills and concepts within this publication are of general comment only and are not recommended as individual advice.

The intent is to offer a variety of information to provide a wider range of choices now and in the future, recognising that we all have widely diverse circumstances and viewpoints.

Should any reader make use of the information contained herein, this is their decision, and the contributors (and their companies), authors and publishers assume no responsibilities under any conditions or circumstances. The reader should obtain their own independent advice.

FIRST EDITION 2020

All rights reserved. No part of this publication may be reproduced, stored in a retrieval system, or transmitted in any form or by means, electronic, mechanical, photocopying, recording or otherwise, without prior written permission from the publisher.

Published by

Job Search Qld

ISBN 978-0-6488025-0-1

Acknowledgements

First, I would like to thank the Universe. In putting this book together, you have given me the power, guidance and clarity to pursue my dreams.

To my best friend, Shari Bertels: You will never know how much you mean to me and I am eternally grateful for your encouragement, love, support and belief in me. Thank you for being in my corner and pushing me when things got tough. Wherever you are in the world, I will always love you and be in your corner. You made so many sacrifices for me to follow my passions and dreams.

To my mother, Christine McLaughlin, and father, Burtland McLaughlin: Thank you for the unconditional love and support you have given me over the years. You have been great role models and I love the nature at which you put family first. You've given me so much and made so many sacrifices. I'm infinitely grateful from the bottom of my heart. I love you both very dearly.

To my brother, Troy McLaughlin: You always made me feel as if you were proud that I was your older brother and that always made me proud to have you as my brother despite all our shortcomings. Thank you for your suggestions, guidance and belief in me. Please know that I love you so much, even when I'm not around.

To Tony Robbins: You have helped change my life and realigned my core values. I am deeply grateful for what you have shown me is possible. I feel extremely lucky to have connected with so many like-minded people at your events and so many are playing the game at a much higher level and are positively affecting the world.

To my Social Media mentor and friend, Kerry Fitzgibbon: I'm immensely grateful to you because you motivated me to produce this book and you also continue to show up and give a great deal of value in a fun way. I absolutely love your sense of humour.

To Tom Bilyeu: You my friend have given me an even greater sense of determination and resilience. I remember listening to your content in the gym at 3am in the morning. I was lucky enough to meet you a few weeks ago in Brisbane. Some concepts that have been ingrained in me now are "Ideas in equals Ideas out" and "It doesn't matter who you are today, it only matters who you want to become and how hard you are willing to work to become that person".

To Kat Abianac, you are an absolute superstar and genius. I honestly can't thank you enough for your time, generosity and openness. I love spending time with you. You have a wealth of knowledge and experience and you share it in such a fun way.

To my Business Coach, Pushpa Chauhan: Thank you for helping me to get my business off the ground and make me accountable for my actions. I'm enormously grateful for you showing me the importance of working on my inner self. Words can't describe how incredible and inspiring you truly are.

A Clever Guide To Winning The Job Interview

To my mentor Aaron Sansoni: You are seriously one of the best presenters and you are extremely talented at what you do. By attending your events, you have truly inspired me and I'm extremely thankful for all the value and strategies that you have taught me.

To my friend and former mentor, Mark Lothian: I seriously can't thank you enough for teaching me about people, sales, controlling my emotions and becoming a man. I'm thankful for the potential you saw in me and the faith you placed in me.

A special mention to Veronica Pollard and Jo McCatty for your time and contribution. Thank you for sharing your recruitment experience, knowledge, ideas and strategies with me. You are both beautiful inside and out, intelligent with a great sense of humour and I love how down to earth and approachable you are. I'm incredibly lucky to have you as friends.

A special mention to Graeme Lammie: You are one of the best recruiters I know. I am grateful to you for your leadership and mentoring. Along with showing me strategies, processes and how to ask quality questions and draw out specific information from candidates.

About The Author

Dre McLaughlin is the Founder and Director of Job Search Qld. A platform to help people kick start their careers and gain the confidence they need to step up onto the next level of their career.

A previous winner of the Australian Annual Sales Award in 2011 for Vodafone business and he has had a successful background in sales and recruitment. Dre has managed accounts and recruited for some of the largest companies in Australia and the world. Companies such as GHD Engineering, National Heart Foundation, Ray White Corporate, St John's Ambulance, Foxtel, Wenatex, Apple Marketing, Michelin, Blue Dog Training and Orora to name a few.

Through his experiences, Dre has built up an affinity and understanding of others with an innate ability to forge genuine, long-lasting relationships. He is resourceful, tenacious and passionate while possessing an energy and enthusiasm for helping people to reach their goals.

Over the years, Dre has participated in thousands and thousands of interviews as an interviewee, but mostly as an interviewer. Conducting interviews with school students all the way up to directors of multinational companies earning high six figure incomes.

Dre is devoted to sharing his knowledge, skills, experience and expertise with the world.

Introduction

Feeling nervous, or anxious about your job interview?

I have found that millions of people are terrified of job interviews and crippled by the fear of interviewing for a job they really want. During the interview, they cannot perform at their best due to either intense anxiety, fear of being negatively evaluated, fear of judgement, or fear of rejection.

Research from the Dale Carnegie Training Company now tells us that the number one fear in the world is not public speaking anymore, but the ability to converse with a stranger. This is especially true for the younger generation. This can be defined as Anthrophobia the fear of people.

So, imagine for a moment, you're sat in an interview, you've just met the hiring manager who is in a position of influence, you're talking about yourself, while worrying whether you're being scrutinised. At the same time, you are being judged on your behaviour, appearance and your ability to sell yourself. All of this can be major factors for suffering extreme social anxiety.

I've been on both sides of the coin. I've been the interviewee many times and the interviewer thousands of times. Some of the reasons I failed interviews and faced rejection was because I was:

- ✘ Paralysed by nerves and extreme sweating
- ✘ Not able to express my ideas and articulate my sentences
- ✘ Not prepared at all
- ✘ Arrived late
- ✘ Turned up an hour early
- ✘ Too much of a nice guy
- ✘ Not confidently able to back up a claim I made about a book I read
- ✘ Not able to state my resume inside out or discuss my sales figures
- ✘ Overconfident and airing on the side of arrogance

Several years ago, I was interviewing for an account management position with Toshiba at their Woolloongabba office in Brisbane. I was being interviewed by two senior managers. During the interview, I had said that I loved reading sales and self-development books.

The interview was one of the best interviews I'd ever had until these last two questions.
"What was the last sales book that you have read?" My response was slightly delayed, I said
"The Psychology of Selling, by Brian Tracy". One interviewer said, "Oh, that's a great book, one of my favourites, what's your favourite part of the book?"

Shock, horror, I wasn't expecting to be asked that question. The funny thing and I guess the worst thing is that I hadn't read the book, but I had listened to the audiobook in my car a week earlier.

It was a tumbleweed moment and for the life of me, I couldn't think of a specific part of the audiobook. I can't remember exactly what I said, but I know it was like a train wreck. Something along the lines of saying I liked the ending of the book and some of the strategies. I gave a very vague answer.

Later that afternoon, I got a call from Vanessa the recruiter and she said that I would not be progressing to the final interview stage, due to the final answers I had given. A good lesson learned, and a great opportunity missed.

You only get one shot to make a good first impression.
The first several seconds of meeting someone are crucial.

The interview should be a free flow of information between people, like a tennis match, back and forth. Questions and answers from both sides with both the interviewer and the interviewee feeling comfortable.

This book has been developed for people who:

- ✓ Want to secure their first job
- ✓ Are scared or fearful about having a job interview
- ✓ Want to get an edge over their competition
- ✓ Have no idea how to prepare for an interview
- ✓ Want to win their dream job
- ✓ Want strategies to shine in their interview

What To Expect

Before you go for your first job interview, you need to understand the interview process. Normally you'll have at least two interviews. The first interview will be with a Recruitment Consultant or the HR Dept (Human Resources).

If they deem you suitable, then they will put you forward to the Manager or Team Leader responsible for making the hiring decision.

This all depends on the size of the company; you may be fortunate enough to have one interview at a smaller company that makes recruitment selections much more quickly.

Or depending on the role, you could have multiple interviews where you meet a range of different people within the team, who'll be assessing your suitability for the company.

The ultimate focus is always making the best decision for the company. **The better you can sell yourself at the interview stage, the quicker you'll be able to start the job** you want.

If you are right out of school with little to no experience, you may be asked to take an aptitude test. This is a systematic way of testing a job candidate's abilities to perform specific tasks and check how they react to a range of different situations.

You are normally told about this when you arrange the interview. The kind of testing you must do will depend upon the position for which you are applying.

For example, an office position this might include a touch-typing test and testing familiarity with numerous administration software packages. You must be prepared to undertake all the essential requirements if you want to be employed by the company.

If the company is genuinely interested in hiring you, they may request for you to undergo a drug and alcohol test. This is not something that usually will occur until they decide they would like to hire you.

It is something you must do before they make you a formal offer of employment. If you take recreational drugs, research measures on how long it will take to clear your system. If the company has random drug tests, you will need to give it up.

3 Stages To The Interview

Stage 1: The Beginning
Find things in common and build rapport with the interviewer.

Stage 2: The Middle
The reason you are there.

Stage 3: The End
Closing off the interview and moving it forward.

Different Types of Job Interviews

There are several different types of job interviews. Essentially the interviewer is attempting to establish if the candidate is a good fit for the position while at the same time selling the company.

Candidates attempt to sell themselves while determining if the company is a good company to work for. First impressions, body language and other non-verbal signs, as well as interview attire are extremely important as well.

The interviewer will normally interview more than one person and you will be compared to those candidates. So, the applicants will create a context for the interviewer in terms of one candidate is better than others.

Depending on the type of interview the questions would be a combination of general, technical, skill and behavioural questions. **The more you know about the style of the interview, the better you can prepare.**

Assessment Centres

Assessment centres are exercises generally used by employers to test skills that are not assessable from the traditional interview approach. The assessment centre is usually the last obstacle in the recruitment process and is where the employer really turns up the heat on the candidates. Assessment centres assess by using role-play scenarios, psychometric tests, personality tests, ability tests and group exercises.

Informal Interviews

Seldom done at entry level, informal interviews are commonplace in sales and leadership roles. There is no reason this should not be a part of the interview process for other roles as well. Conversations about new job opportunities happen over breakfast, lunch, or dinner.

These informal settings, such as coffee catch-ups, help break the ice. There are no written rules that say interviews must be conducted in a conference room or office. One thing of which you must be careful allowing the informal setting to detract from the purpose of the meeting.

You are there to discuss a job opening and have simply chosen to do so informally rather than in the interviewer's office. This type of situation works well for those people who are averse to formal meetings, or where the interviewer may not want someone in the office to know he or she is looking for additional staff. The new person could be there to replace someone already failing at their job.

Informal arrangements can be very helpful for those who have not had an interview in a long time or have just graduated and are a little nervous about entering the industry of their choice. It's easy enough to provide a relaxing atmosphere in which you can talk without being disturbed by visitors or by telephone calls.

Formal Interviews

A formal interview is a meeting between a potential job candidate and the prospective employer.

Formal interviews can be conducted in any business or trade.

Formal interviews are traditional and the most common form of interviewing.

Phone interviews

A phone interview is typically called a screening interview and the first stage in the interview process. Usually, a phone interview includes a brief review of your experience and you'll be asked questions intended to determine if you're a suitable candidate for the position. Phone interviews tend to last between 10 to 20 minutes.

When you have a phone interview, the interviewer can't see your facial expressions, hand gestures or other body language signals.

The tone of your voice is vital, so make sure you sound enthusiastic, engaged and interested.

Let your personality shine through. The interviewer wants to get a feel for who you are as a person.

- ✓ If you have a phone interview booked in, find out how long the interview time is planned for.

- ✓ Find a quiet place where you won't be interrupted. The worst thing is when an interviewer can hear screaming kids, animals, or other loud noises in the background. It comes across as very unprofessional.

- ✓ I used to find that when I was a bit nervous on the phone, I would forget what I wanted to say, or wouldn't be able to get my point across in the right manner. **Print a copy of your resume out so you have it in hand,** and you can refer to it if you get lost words.

- ✓ Have a notepad ready to jot down any notes or questions you might think of.

- ✓ Start with saying, "Thank you for taking time out of your busy schedule to talk with me today. I've been looking forward to this call".

- ✓ Know the details of the job you have applied for. If you have a copy of a job description, read that fully and have a copy printed out so you can refer to it if needed.

- ✓ Candidates I coach, I tell them that **interviewers can "hear your smile" over the phone.** Consider how you sound when you talk about something exciting with one of your friends.

- ✓ **Stand up when you're on the call,** this places a reduced amount of tension on your diaphragm than sitting down. Your voice will be clearer and **psychologically, you'll feel more confident** and in control. You're more likely to embrace a natural form of dialogue.

- ✓ Be prepared to talk about salary. The interviewer may ask you what your salary expectations are. So, make sure you have done your research into what the industry is paying for the role you are applying for.

- ✓ Towards the end of the interview, always ask about the next steps, so when you are likely to hear back whether you have succeeded to the next interview stage.
  Always, always, always thank the interviewer for their time.

Video/ Virtual/ Online Job Interviews

A virtual interview, also known as digital or video interview, allows people to conduct an interview in an automatic manner by conducting it online.

The interviewers use a virtual interview as a standard way of assessing the potential of the candidates.

A one-way video interview is an asynchronous video interview in which job candidates record video responses to interview questions in their own time.

One-way video interviews are also called pre-recorded video interviews because they don't require the interviewer to be present.

On the day of the interview, dress professionally, wearing the same interview attire you would for an in-person interview. While the camera angle should show you from the waist up (your face is the real focal point), if there is any possibility you will need to stand up, make sure you are wearing pants or a skirt and it's professional.

Tips for a virtual interview:

- ✓ **Double-check your audio, video, and internet connection** an hour or two before your scheduled interview time

- ✓ Pick a plain or distraction-free background

- ✓ Dress for the job you want

- ✓ Make sure you're in a well-lit room and the interviewer can see you clearly

- ✓ Keep your body language open

- ✓ Keep your hands in view

- ✓ Angle and eye contact are critical

- ✓ Frame yourself from the chest up

Group Interviews

Employers conduct group interviews to see how candidates engage and interact in unfamiliar environments. Employers may have many candidates for the same role and instead of having individual interviews, they group people so they can disregard those who are not right for the position.

Doing it this way saves a huge amount of time. Most people become rather shy and timid in this kind of situation. People are less reluctant to discuss previous employment experience in front of a group of people they don't know.

The strategy for this type of interview is to **find the right balance of being extroverted and introverted.** In this type of interview, you will be watched as soon as you walk through the building door, or even earlier.

Be the first one to introduce yourself to people, such as the receptionist, other people that might be interviewing with you, other employees and the cleaners. Do this in a way where you are not being overly loud.

Open body language, communication and the way you interact with others is extremely important. Make sure you listen to other people and respond accordingly and encourage other people to join in and participate in any discussions.

One on One Interviews

The one to one job interview is the most common style of interview, where only the interviewer and the interviewee are present.

The structure of the interview is where the interviewer is directing the discussion initially and the interviewee is asking questions towards the end.

The best way is to have a conversational type interview, back and forth with questions and answers from both sides, so it's a flow of information.

If you can **control the interview in a subtle way**, you're 90% there to landing the job of your dreams.

Panel Interviews

Panel interviews are conducted by a group of two to five people, sometimes more. Often, you'll be in a room with several people who work at the company and these interviewers make up the panel.

Your panel of interviewers will represent multiple areas of the company, and they will come from different backgrounds and roles. Each of them will view your resume and responses in a different way.

Companies like this style of interview because it saves a huge amount of time. The company can book one interview instead of coordinating several one-on-one meetings. It allows all the company's representatives to reach an agreement before making a hiring decision.

Panel interviews can be extremely nerve-racking and intimidating. To prepare for this style of interview. Find out who will be present at your interview. Ask your company contact to give you a bit of background information on each of the panel.

Your opening introductions with the panel will be crucial. If you're terrible at remembering names, you will need to flip your mindset. Tell yourself that you are great at remembering names.

To really stand out from the crowd and impress during the interview, **you must remember and use each interviewer's name** and role throughout the meeting.

If you're adamant you won't be able to remember and recite the panel's names, at the start of the interview, **ask the interviewers if they mind if you take down some notes.** This is almost always acceptable.

Once you know who's who in the zoo, you can build rapport by connecting and engaging with the interviewers as a group and individually.

Answer each question precisely while adding points to tackle the different viewpoints of the other interviewers. For example, one interviewer might ask you about how you work effectively within a team.

Other department managers will be more concerned with how you would engage with their teams. So, you could say something like, "Working effectively in a team is a necessity; everyone should have clearly defined roles and responsibilities. This helps to improve communication within the team and collaboration across other teams".

When replying, direct your answer to the person who asked the question, as you continue to go into detail and provide examples, **address the rest of the panel by making eye contact, moving your shoulders so that you're directly facing each person.**

If they look down and make notes, continue to shift your gaze from person to person to create a more relaxed environment.

This is a great way to boost your rapport with the group, by taking a question and moulding it to apply to each person on the panel instead of just the person that asked the question.

Be prepared for rapidly firing questions and follow-up questions from multiple people.

Remember to take a slight pause, think about what you will say, then deliver your answer.

You'll most likely get another question thrown at you before you have even finished answering your current question.

Potential Interviews From Job Searching

Don't search for a job wearing jeans or shorts. If you're picking up applications from retail stores, or small businesses, you risk one employee will recognize you as someone who came in to pick up an application form and they, will relay their opinion of you to the manager.

You'll probably be wondering why you didn't get the call. If people are not like you, they can make snap negative judgements about you, without knowing the real you.

If you go out with the sole purpose to look for employment, dress appropriately just in case the company does on the spot interviews. You don't want to kill your chances of being hired because you failed to plan accordingly.

Don't take a friend with you unless the friend is providing transport, or also job searching. There is no need for your friend to go inside the building with you and hold your hand. Ask them to meet you at a nearby coffee shop.

Booking The Interview

When you call to schedule an interview, there are likely to be other candidates that also want to book interviews. Although, it is more common for employers to call and book in with candidates they are interested in.

If you are interested in securing employment, you must **be willing to compromise with interview times** so it's convenient for both sides.

If you do not want your current employer to know you are looking for something else, you may have to think of an excuse, or just state you have some personal business to which you must attend rather than lie about why you need the time off.

In these cases, you are usually notified about the time and if it runs for an hour, you can be sure your interview will be within that period.

Do not be afraid to tell the interviewer you have something scheduled at such and such a time so you can work around that schedule.

Often, if the interviewer knows you have other interviews and if they really want you, they will make a quick decision to hire you. This practice was more common in the past than it is now, but it still happens.

To avoid potential conflicts, limit your interviews to two a day. One in the morning and one in the afternoon with a gap of at least four to five hours between them.

You do not want to over-schedule and then sit there fidgeting while trying to hope you can make the second interview on time. Not only is this kind of behaviour distracting to the interviewer who will be able to sense you are trying to rush, but it will also cause you to take your focus off what the interviewer is saying while you attempt to rush things along.

A Professional Voicemail & Email Address

It is absolutely critical that you have a professional voicemail and email address if you want to be taken seriously. I've worked with so many young people with inappropriate voicemails.

I admit some are funny. However, a hiring manager will rule you out of the running for a job. Record your message in an upbeat, positive tone.

Say something like...

"Hello! You've reached the voicemail of [your name], I'm currently away from my phone or on another call.

Please leave your name, telephone number, and a short message, and I'll be sure to call you back as soon as possible."

Having a professional email address is critical in today's job market. Thousands of people submit their resume or CV using unsuitable email addresses.

Your email address should be your name, or as close to it as possible – for example, John.Smith@gmail.com or JohnSmith88@hotmail.com.

Multiple Interview Invitations

If you have sent out countless resumes and you're lucky enough to get multiple requests for you to come in for an interview.

It is vital that you choose the right job opportunities to interview for. If you're not currently working, then this isn't an issue. If you're studying or employed, you will have limited time.

How do you choose from these interview requests?

Choose the opportunities closely aligned with what you want to do. When you're against the clock, it's crucial to choose those interviews highly beneficial to your career.

If you have several possibilities that may be good career choices, you might need to weigh up all your options.

If you limit yourself to a specific number of interviews, you may have a challenging time finding the position you want. Avoid requests for interviews that do not directly promote your choice of a career. Be selective and look to the best career options to reduce your interview time.

Research The Company & Industry

If you are interviewing with a company unknown to you, carry out some research. In almost every interview, the interviewer will ask you what you know about the company?

Or what you feel you can bring to the company, and these can be very difficult questions to answer if you know nothing about the business.

You can learn a great deal of information by searching Google and looking at:

- ✓ Company Websites
- ✓ Facebook
- ✓ Instagram
- ✓ Tik Tok
- ✓ Twitter
- ✓ LinkedIn
- ✓ YouTube
- ✓ Annual Reports
- ✓ Current Projects
- ✓ New Articles
- ✓ Customer Testimonials
- ✓ Glass Door Reviews
- ✓ If you know anyone in the company use them as leverage for inside information

If you do not have access to a mobile phone, PC at home or work, go to your local library and look up some information on the company.

By doing your research, this will show you are genuine, motivated and this will give you the edge at crunch time, when a decision is to be made between you and someone else who hasn't done their research.

A few little one percent increments throughout the interview process will add up to make a huge difference.

The more you learn about the company, the better-educated decision you can make on whether you will be a good fit for the team. The interviewer can only tell you so much about the company and culture as you don't always get a clear picture.

On occasions, there may not be enough time to carry out a great deal of research, but you need to collect enough information to show the interviewer you have at least heard of the company and know what products and services they offer.

Please be aware it's also important to find out about what causes the company is involved in. For example, they may support a controversial type of research, which you disagree with. You can save time with the hiring process by avoiding choosing a company that doesn't align with your values.

Research The Interviewer

If you know the name of the person that will be interviewing you, **STALK THEM!!!** That's right, I said **STALK THEM!!!** Not literally but in the social media sense.

Put your investigator hat on and search through:

- ✓ Company Website
- ✓ Facebook
- ✓ Instagram
- ✓ Tik Tok
- ✓ Twitter
- ✓ LinkedIn
- ✓ YouTube
- ✓ New Articles
- ✓ Customer Testimonials
- ✓ Glass Door Reviews

If you can find any information on them, this will help tell you what type of person they are and it's **easier to build rapport** with someone. This will help to **make you stand out from the crowd.**

For example, if you **see that the interviewer is playing Golf in one of their social media photos. That's a great conversation starter or a brilliant way to demonstrate that you have done your research.**

James (interviewer) when I was doing my research, I came across a photo of you playing golf.

- How often do you play?
- Where do you play?

If the interviewer is passionate about it, they will have a smile on their face, and open up and talk about it for a while.

If you play golf as well, then it's a great way to find a common interest and develop the relationship. If you can keep the interviewer talking more than you can, that's half the battle won.

'When doing your research on the interviewer, look for things that you have in common so you can leverage off it in the interview'.

Do You Know The Interview Process?

Every business has its own interview process. Familiarize yourself with the interview process for the company you will be interviewing for. The larger organisations let their HR Department handle the whole interview process from start to finish.

In most companies, the HR Dept only does the preliminary interview and presents the best-qualified candidates to the manager who makes the final decision. Nowadays, it is very rare to be hired on the spot unless you are an absolute superstar with multiple job offers on the table.

In larger organisations, you'll usually have at least two interviews. One with Human Resources and one with the Department Manager/Direct Supervisor. Sometimes this can happen on the same day.

If the HR department are working to a tight deadline and feel you are qualified for the position, they will get you to meet the department manager while you're already there. If this happens, leave ample time if you are booking more than one interview in one day. It's not always true that your interview will be finished within an hour.

Always allow for at least two hours, not including travel time. Plan for no more than two interviews in a day unless you are 100% certain that you will only spend an hour at each interview.

Do You Know Your Resume Inside Out?

Not knowing your resume will cost you the job and place you in an embarrassing situation. Your resume is a tool that supported getting you the interview. Interviewers use your resume as a starting point to ask you questions around your skills, knowledge and previous work experience.

This approach helps the interviewer establish your creditability. If you cannot speak about your resume clearly, in detail and without hesitation, the interviewer will feel as though you are lying and have fabricated some, or all of the information.

Millions of people fail interviews because they don't have accurate information on their resume. Experienced recruiters and hiring managers can work out if a candidate is truthful.

Here are some example questions interviewers have asked based on information in resumes:

- ✓ "I see you're fluent in German, do you mind if we conduct the rest of this interview in German?"

- ✓ "You state on your resume you increased sales by 175%, what sales amount was that increase based on and how did you accomplish this increase?"

- ✓ "On your resume, you claim you're very analytical and mathematical. One plus one half plus one fourth plus one eighth gets closer to a certain number; what is the number and why?"

- ✓ "You had in an internship in the UK for three months, what part of the UK did you stay in, tell me about how your living there differs from Australia?"

- ✓ "You state you won first prize nationally for an article you wrote, where can I find this article and is it published online?"

Do You Want To Get Over Your Nerves & Feel More Confident?

Fear and excitement generate the same emotions and the brain goes through the same chemical process with both feelings.

Here are a few strategies to help you embrace those feelings, control them and use them to your advantage, so you can perform at your best in the interview.

- ✓ **Visualization** is a technique of seeing an image of yourself that you are proud of, in your own mind. When we battle with low self-esteem, we have a poor opinion of ourselves that is often inaccurate.

    Practice visualizing the best version of yourself, achieving interview success and focus on the feeling you'll have when you win the job.

- ✓ **Affirmations** are positive statements that can help you to challenge and overcome self-sabotaging and negative thoughts. When you repeat them out loud and often, and believe in them, you can make positive changes.

Examples of affirmations you could use:

- ✓ I am confident
- ✓ I am successful
- ✓ I am resilient
- ✓ I am engaging
- ✓ I am resourceful
- ✓ I am tenacious

- ✓ **Practice your interview answers** and be prepared the best you can be.

- ✓ **Looking sharp for an interview** makes you feel good because it makes you feel like you can do anything.

- ✓ **Use a Power Stance. Practicing confident body** language is another way to boost your confidence. When your body is physically demonstrating confidence, your mind will follow.

  Studies have shown that using power stances a few minutes before going to an interview creates a lasting sense of confidence.

- ✓ My personal favourite is **doing press-ups or running on the spot** to get the blood pumping around the body.

  I usually do this before presenting to large audiences and I've done this countless times before interviews.

  Everybody is different, so choose the method that works for you.

- ✓ Sit up straight in the interview. When people sit up straight, they are more inclined to believe in themselves and that they are qualified for the job.

  When other people look at us sitting upright, they get a positive impression we appear confident.

- ✓ **Box breathing is a Navy SEAL technique for reducing stress.** Before your meeting, take deep breaths by breathing in for 4 seconds, holding for 4 seconds and out for 4 seconds for and repeat that 5-6 times.

  Besides the positive physiological impact, having to focus on your breaths gives your brain a direct experience.

- ✓ A few minutes before you step into the interview, slow down. Be more present and in the moment. Walk slower to the building. Move slower. Even stop for a minute if you like and stand still.

- ✓ Music can raise people's moods, excite them, or make them feel calm and relaxed. It improves memory, attention, physical coordination and concentration.

    So, put on your favourite tunes that resonate with the feeling you want to have. **'Rock Out or Chill Out'.**

- ✓ **Everybody gets rejected.** It sucks! Fearing rejection will pile on the pressure and boost your nerves.

    So many famous people have been rejected numerous times. People such as Oprah, Walt Disney, Michael Jordan, Beyoncé, J.K. Rowling, Albert Einstein and Lady Gaga to name a few.

    Rejection is something that happens to all of us; don't let it weaken your value. So, you didn't get the job you really wanted. Learn from the experience and move on. **Often, a better opportunity is right around the corner.**

A Clever Guide To Winning The Job Interview

"Get Comfortable Being Uncomfortable"

How To Avoid These Common Interview Mistakes

It is important when looking to secure a position when jobs are limited to **present yourself in the best possible light**. Job hunters continually make several common mistakes that often cost them the position.

Educating yourself and avoiding these pitfalls will significantly increase your chances for a successful interview and the job. It's not rocket science, but it requires some commitment and understanding of the importance. Once you know what you are doing wrong, you can change it, so your next interview will be much smoother.

Dressing inappropriately is one of the first things that will cost you a successful interview. You may think it is acceptable to wear a t-shirt and jeans to an interview because you don't have any dress clothes.

The truth is that jeans are not at all acceptable attire for any interview. Unless your interview takes place at a construction site, or in a warehouse and then only if the interviewer tells you, prior to the interview that the location will be dirty.

A Clever Guide To Winning The Job Interview

If you have tattoos, I suggest covering them up and take out any visible piercings. If you are having an interview with someone from an older generation (OK Boomer), they will make a judgement call about you and take the view of how you might come across at first glance, to their clients.

If the interview is with a younger person, they are more understanding and will probably have several tattoos themselves. The goal is for you to get your foot in the door by way of them offering you the job.

There is never an acceptable time to wear shorts to an interview, not even a shorts outfit. The only appropriate attire for an interview unless otherwise instructed by the company with which you are interviewing is skirts, blouses, dresses and trousers with coordinating tops for the ladies and trousers with collared shirts and suits for the men.

Always overdress than underdress. Remember you're competing for the position, **'SO DRESS TO IMPRESS'**.

For example, if it's a stinking hot day, which it usually is in Queensland, and you're a guy wearing a suit with a tie, you can always ask to take the tie, or jacket off during the interview.

Almost all interviewers will understand how uncomfortable you will be in that situation. **It's that first impression, the first several seconds that really count.**

Bringing a mobile phone to the interview is something else that will cost you a successful interview. If you cannot leave your phone in the car, at least have the courtesy to turn it off, or put it in silent mode.

Unless it's a life-threatening emergency with one of your children or family members, nothing cannot wait until the interview is complete.

Instruct friends and family to avoid contacting you until you are finished with your interview. During your interview, you should not even have your mobile phone in your hand or within your view.

You should not use your mobile phone during an interview. On top of this, never ever bring children to an interview.

Interview Guidelines

If you want to improve your odds of securing the job, you must know what is appropriate and what is not when you go for the interview.

They may seem like small things to a job seeker, however doing the right things at the right time can make a huge impact on getting hired.

It's crucial to know what things may earn you extra brownie points and those that will cost you the job opportunity.

Most people are aware of what to do and what not do during an interview; for those of you looking for your first full-time job, you may not be aware.

Things to do before, during and after your interview

- ✓ Research the company

- ✓ **Research the interviewer** if you know their name

- ✓ **Have at least 3 copies of your resume printed out**

- ✓ Have suitable clothing for an interview (professional or business casual depending on the company), freshly laundered and pressed or hung to dry to remove wrinkles

- ✓ **Prepare a list of quality questions** to ask at the interview

- ✓ **Have a notebook** to take notes during the interview

- ✓ **Be on time** for the interview. If there are circumstances beyond your control, call the interviewer and give him or her the option to still see you, or reschedule the interview

- ✓ **Turn off your mobile phone** or put it in silent mode

- ✓ **Send a 'Thank You' note, email or text** to the interviewer as soon as possible after the interview. This increases your chances of being hired.

Things not to do before or during the interview

- Do not schedule interviews too close together in case there are additional things you need to do, such as testing or meeting with the department manager

- Do not bring your children or anyone else with you to an interview unless they are also applying for a position

- Never smoke during an interview even if you can do so and if you smoke right before the interview have gum, or breath mints for your mouth and spray to remove the smell from your clothing

- Never snack or chew gum. If you use gum or mints to kill the taste of cigarette smoke, finish them before you go in for the interview

- Stay on topic during the interview and avoid personal discussions

- Do not bring drinks into the interview. **Only bring a small bottle of water** and ask the interviewer if they mind if you bring it into the meeting.

If the interviewer offers you tea, or coffee, say "no thank you". First, it's very off-putting if you are loudly slurping your hot drink while they are asking you questions.

Second, it's awkward if the interview has finished and you're quickly trying to finish your hot drink while exiting the room.

The reason I say to **have water in the meeting is because it gives you time to think** if the interviewer is asking you a difficult question and you can't think of what to say.

Take a sip of water slowly (not too slowly that it's obvious) and this will allow you more time.

If you still can't think of an answer by the time you put your glass down. Ask the interviewer to repeat the question.

Are You Prepared For The Interview?

If you have emailed your resume, it is a good idea to bring three additional copies with you. Often, an interviewer will begin by asking questions about information on your resume, and it is much easier for you to follow along if you have a copy of your resume with you.

In addition, many interviewers want a fresh copy of your resume. They have usually made many notes on the copy they have and would like a fresh, crisp copy to view during the interview.

Choose your clothing a few days before the interview so you have time to wash, dry clean and iron anything that may be wrinkled. Be careful of the colours you choose; you should never choose bright colours that take attention away from you.

Dark and pastel shades are preferred and choose styles that are conservative and not too revealing. Although this applies more to women than men do, it is a point that is worth repeating.

You want the interviewer to look at you and not at your cleavage, so even if you are well endowed, do not think you can use it to win over the interviewer even if it's a guy.

Have a notebook to take notes. Even if you have a list of questions you have prepared, there will be some points you will want to recall for later, especially the interviewer's name so you can send a "Thank you" note, email or text.

Depending on the kind of job you're interviewing for, it will be valuable to **bring a portfolio of your past work**, achievements, awards, etc.

This can be a folder or even a website shown on your laptop, or tablet. Your portfolio should be organised so it's easy to refer to during your interview.

Confirm with your referees and ask them if they will be a point of contact for employers seeking to verify or ask questions about your background, work experience, or work ethic.

You can provide both professional and personal references to a potential employer. If they won't give you a glowing reference, use someone else. You can ask a former teacher, former employer, supervisor, sports team coach or manager.

Personal & Professional Social Media Profiles

Social media is a key player in the job search process. Websites and Apps like Facebook, Twitter, Tik Tok, LinkedIn, and Instagram allow employers to get an indication of who you are external from the limitations of your resume, cover letter, or interview:

- ✓ Photos and social media posts with lewd themes can hinder a job search.

- ✓ Cleaning up your Facebook, Instagram, Twitter, LinkedIn, Tik Tok and other apps that could attract attention from potential employers. Employers will do a social media stalk on you too.

- ✓ Maintain a **professional online presence** with professional looking photos and text.

The Law of Reciprocity

When doing your research, if you see a picture on Instagram or Facebook of the interviewer and/or the team enjoying chocolates, donuts, fruit, or something else, you can leverage off this.

Buy a box of goodies and bring it along to the interview and when you hand it to the interviewer, say this is for them and the team to share and enjoy. Give them a warm, cheeky smile and say, "Yes, I am trying to score brownie points".

You are not guaranteed to get the job and if you do narrowly miss out on the role, they will remember you and may recommend you to another department or other company. **I can guarantee you that you will definitely stand out from the crowd.**

"People won't always remember what you said, but they will remember the way you made them feel".

Social psychologists call it "The law of reciprocity". **When someone does something nice for you, you will have a deep-rooted psychological urge to do something nice for them in return.** Often, the other person will reciprocate with a deed far more generous than their original gesture.

Control The Conversation

Another problem that people face is not being able to control the conversation during an interview, so it follows a professional flow. Trying to engage the interviewer in personal conversation may not give you brownie points.

Sometimes, it may cause you to lose credibility because it will appear as though you are attempting to obtain the job by making friends with the interviewer.

Interviewers are not perfect; there are numerous times when they will talk about personal topics. **Be very, very careful** because some hiring managers will set out to lower your guard and entice you to let your guard down, so you feel comfortable and they will extract personal information from you by manipulating the conversation away from professionalism. Dodge these kinds of discussions and stay on topic. Recruiters are exceptionally good at doing this.

You don't want to overrun the interviewer's time and not be able to find out everything you need to know about the position and the company. It is okay to mention your family but there is no need to go into detail and the interviewer shouldn't ask.

If you have young children and the question arises about childcare, all you need to say is that it is taken care of.

If you comprise a list of quality questions to ask the interviewer, you will side-step delving into personal conversations. You will be focused on asking questions and taking in the interviewer's answers while thinking of further questions at the same time.

The key is to remain on topic. Through keeping the discussions on topic, you can close out the interview on time and have answers to all the questions you thought of. After the interview, you will feel more comfortable about which way the interview went.

At the start of the interview, if the employer hasn't mentioned the type of person they are looking for, ask them. So you get more of an insight than what is listed on the job description. Throughout the interview and when you close off the interview, **use the same words back to the interviewer**, demonstrating that you are the outstanding candidate they have been looking for.

Verbal Communication - Be Careful What You Say & How You Say It

One of my favourite sayings is, **"Words change lives"**. When speaking with someone about a new role, regardless of whether it is the same company you work for, be careful about your choice of words.

Millions of people squander great opportunities because they fail to follow stringent grammatical and professional correct language during an interview. If you are not used to using correct grammar, it's essential you use it during a job interview.

It's okay to use slang when talking to friends and co-workers, however, in an interview, you must speak as though you are well educated.

Never under any circumstances, use slang or swearwords in an interview. If normally every other word is a swearword, think very carefully before speaking. The interviewer's office is not an acceptable place for this type of language.

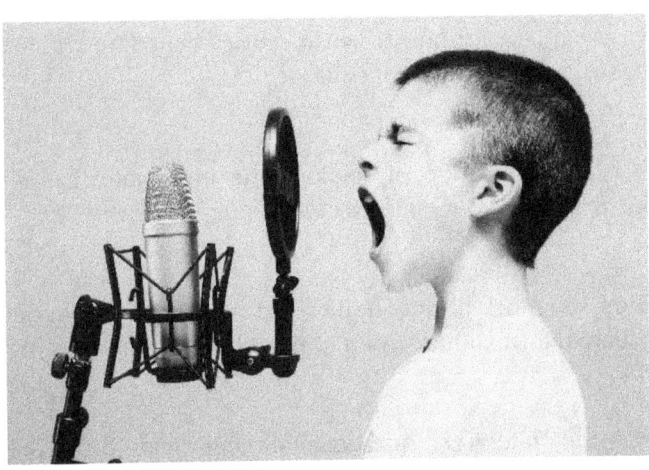

Your choice of words can alter whether you are chosen for the job. If you're unsure about your grammar skills, take some time to learn common word choices before you go to your interview. Using incorrect verbs or slang will be noticeable.

Choose your words so you present yourself as a professional rather than somebody who needs to go back to school to improve their English. **Don't try to make yourself look more intelligent by using big words you don't understand.** You will look like an idiot and it will cost you the job.

How Much Should You Share During the Interview?

Knowing how much information you should provide in an interview can be enormously hard to gage. When we are nervous or anxious, it is so easy to overshare.

Don't fall into the trap of thinking the more information you provide the better your chances are of being chosen.

Providing too much information will throw a negative light on you. Only share information relevant to the job you're interviewing for.

Answer the interview questions directly and only provide information related to the position. If you were fired from a previous job and the interviewer doesn't ask you about it, keep your mouth shut, you are under no obligation to provide that information.

Often, the interviewer will only be concerned about your previous jobs that relate to the position you are applying for. Most companies are not checking references like they used to do twenty years ago.

Under the Age Discrimination Act 2004, it is unlawful to discriminate against people because of their age. The Equality Act 2010 states it is unlawful for employers to treat you unfairly because of who you are.

Employers are not supposed to ask personal questions about your age or personal circumstances during the interview. However, many employers will ask, and the candidates normally are none the wiser. Once you are hired, these things will be important for insurance purposes.

Employers are also not permitted to ask about children, or childcare arrangements because in the past women with children were often rejected for employment. Due to concerns about who was caring for the children and who would care for them on school holidays.

The more information you reveal, the more reasons you give a potential employer to eliminate your name from qualified candidates. Some may still enquire, however you are under no obligation to discuss your family arrangements unless they are needed for insurance purposes after you win the job.

Practice Makes Permanent, Not Perfect

Never ever go into a job interview expecting to wing it. I've done that before and it cost me the job. I couldn't craft well thought out answers and I forgot things I wanted to say.

Practice does not make perfect, but it is sure to make it better. **Practicing for job interviews result in better real interviews.** The more interviews you do, the more skilled you will be at doing them.

Go to your first interview with the poise that comes with having done five or six interviews by engaging a friend, family member, or **Job Search Qld offer a free 10-15 minute online practice interview with you, which is recorded, and you are given verbal feedback and a copy of the recording.**

This practice mimics the process of an interview from the time you walk through the door until you leave the interview. Practice answering common interview questions

Feeling unprepared increases anxiety. Nothing's more embarrassing than having to battle for answers, or to be at a loss for any meaningful questions. Give yourself a helping hand and practice what you will say during an interview.

Avoid using a script. The best approach is to practice with talking points so you can rehearse answering the questions naturally. You want to appear like a human and not a robot.

Use The Interviewers Name In Conversation

Millions of people fail to remember the names of people they have just met. **Remembering names is important.** People will feel they are important to you if you remember their name. It makes people feel valued and helps them to be more comfortable speaking with you.

Remembering and calling someone by their name demonstrates a greater connection to who that person is. People hearing their own name is one of the sweetest sounds to the subconscious mind.

For example, you could use their name in the interview conversation like this:

- ✓ "Sarah, great to meet you".
- ✓ "That's a great question, Sarah".
- ✓ "Sarah, can I ask you a question".
- ✓ "That's an interesting question, Sarah".
- ✓ "Sarah, how did you get your start in the company".

How To Answer Challenging Behavioural Interview Questions?

The **STAR** method is a structured approach to answering challenging behavioural based interview questions, by discussing the specific situation, task, action, and result of the situation you are describing.

STAR METHOD

When you're faced with questions of this nature. A helpful technique to use is the STAR method:

S stands for **SITUATION**

What is the background or nature of the problem you encountered?

T stands for **TASK**

What was required of you to mitigate the problem?

A stands for **ACTION**

What did you do in that situation?

R stands for **RESULT**

What was the outcome of your action?

STAR Method Example

Share an example of a time when you faced a difficult problem at school/work.
How did you solve this problem?

Situation "I was working as a customer service assistant at a retail shop. A customer purchased a shirt online and had it delivered to the store.

Task One of my colleagues mistakenly put the shirt on the rack in the shop front floor, another customer purchased it.

Action Before calling the customer to let her know about the accident, I located the same shirt at another shop close by. I arranged to collect it and bring it to the store before they came to collect it the next day. I left the shirt with a gift card to thank them for their understanding.

Result The customer was so grateful, they gave us a 5-star review on Google."

Once you perfect the Star method, the structure is invisible to the listener and it comes across as a well-articulated example.

Create several examples of answers in this format in advance, so you are not struggling on the day and it appears flawless.

What Is Emotional Intelligence?

Emotional intelligence (EQ) is the ability to identify and manage your emotions, as well as other people's emotions.

If you're emotionally intelligent, you can:

- ✓ Self-Awareness:
  Understand your own strengths and weaknesses, and how your actions affect others

- ✓ Self-Regulation:
  Reveal your emotions and exercise restraint when needed

- ✓ Motivation:
  Be self-motivated, resilient, optimistic and driven by inner ambition

- ✓ Empathy:
  Show compassion and connection on an emotional level

- ✓ People Skills:
  Build rapport and trust quickly with others in your team

Many companies now look for people with a high EQ; it's vital for managers and other business leaders to operate in emotionally intelligent ways to meet the needs of today's workers.

Do You Know How To Mirror and Match To Build Rapport?

Body Language is the conscious and unconscious movements and postures by which attitudes and feelings are communicated. A nonverbal communication in which physical behaviours, as opposed to words.

Examples of this, is your body posture, facial expressions, hand gestures, eye movement and use of touch and space.

There have been thousands of studies about the breakdown of communication. In the 1960s, Professor Albert Mehrabian and colleagues at the University of California, Los Angles (UCLA), conducted studies into human communication patterns.

What they found was verbal communication was only 7%, where non- verbal communication contributed to 93%.

If you break the 93% down further, it consists of 55% of your physiology the way you move your body, and 38% is how you use your tone voice.

Your body language in an interview and how you conduct yourself plays a major part in your interview.

Use Mirror and Matching to help Build Rapport with an Interviewer

In the 1970's Neuro-Linguistic Programming, or NLP was created by Richard Bandler and John Grinder. It is an interpersonal communication model.

The concept is that people feel most at ease around people like them. They feel understood. The more somebody believes you are like them, the easier it is to develop trust, build rapport and grow a relationship at the unconscious level.

Mirroring is the simultaneous copying of behaviour of another person, as if reflecting their movements back to them. When done the right way, mirroring generates a positive feeling and receptiveness in you and others.

Matching, in contrast, can have a bit of a delay in time. For example, if an interviewer uncrosses their legs and leans slightly towards you while speaking, you should wait for a few seconds and then discretely take on the same posture.

- ✓ Is your interviewer sitting, relaxing or slouching?
- ✓ Are his/her legs or arms crossed?
- ✓ Is he/she leaning in any certain direction?
- ✓ Are his/her feet together or apart?
- ✓ Is he/she holding anything, such as a pen or glass of water?

If your interviewer crosses his/her legs or places they're hands on a table, wait for about 5 seconds, then match them in the same way. The same applies to shifting to another position, hand placement, etc. Watch how the interviewer moves.

If he or she moves quickly and you move slowly, your patterns are out of sync. Adjust your speed, slightly faster or slow down until you're both comfortable with one another.

The next time you're with your friends, just watch what they and you do. You'll naturally adopt the same stances, postures and behaviours. It's because you are aligned and comfortable around each other.

To charmingly pace and match gestures, observe each in context.

- ✓ Does your interviewer gesture with his/her hands in a certain way, or with a nod or tilt of her head?

- ✓ Are hand gestures exaggerated and expansive, or protective and restrictive?

- ✓ Subtly mirror the gestures of the person you're listening to.

- ✓ If they lean their head to the left, wait a few seconds and lean your head to the right.

Tone: Voice matching is most effective when done indirectly. Subtle adjustments in your tone, rate, volume so it's more like your interviewers. Your mirrored voice should never be drastically different from your own.

Speech Rate: Matching the pace of your interviewer creates a sense of alignment and allows you to more easily **match their energy level.** Your matching pace should be subtle and natural. If you're inherently a slower, more deliberate speaker, you might consider just speeding it up a bit to reduce the gap between the interviewer and yourself.

Examples of Nonverbal Communication Skills

Review this list of nonverbal skills and work on any areas where you think you could improve.

- ✓ Avoid slouching. **Sit with your back straight up against the chair** or lean slightly forward to convey engagement.

- ✓ Steer clear of smiles or laughter when messages are serious.

- ✓ **Display some animation with your hands and facial expressions to project a dynamic presence.** Avoid talking with your hands excessively, which can appear unprofessional. No Jazz hands.

- ✓ Don't bring your phone or anything else that could distract you during an interview or meeting.

- ✓ Eliminate fidgeting and shaking of limbs.

- ✓ Establish frequent but not continuous or piercing eye contact with interviewers.

- ✓ Focus on the conversation.

- ✓ In a **panel or group interview, shift eye contact to the various speakers.**

- ✓ **Introduce yourself with a smile and a firm handshake.** Be sure that your palms are dry.

- ✓ Keep your hands away from your face and hair.

- ✓ Listen carefully and do not interrupt.

- ✓ Maintain open arms; folded arms can convey defensiveness even though that may not be the case.

- ✓ Adjust your vocal tone to express excitement and punctuate key points.

- ✓ Nod to demonstrate understanding.

- ✓ **Observe the reaction of others to your statements.**

- ✓ Read the nonverbal signals of others. Provide clarification if they look confused and wrap up if they have heard enough.

- ✓ Refrain from forced laughter in response to humour.

- ✓ **Avoid looking at the clock, your phone,** or displaying any other signs of disinterest.

- ✓ Respect personal space preferred by your communication partners.

- ✓ **Smile to indicate that you are amused or pleased with the conversation.**

- ✓ Stay calm even when you're nervous.

- ✓ Steer clear of monotone delivery.

- ✓ **Wait until the person is done talking to respond.**

- ✓ **Actively listen**

- ✓ **Tilt your head ever so slightly to the left; it shows that you're interested.** You naturally do it when engaged and interested.

- ✓ There's an old myth that if you look into a person's left eye when interviewing, it means you're connecting to their emotional side, as that's the side of the brain that handles emotion. If you look mainly at the person's right eye, then it is believed that you are demonstrating your dominance. This is something that you should never do in an interview

How to Ensure Interview Success?

Interviewing for a job can be one of the most frightening and challenging things you do. All you need to do is follow some guidelines and trust the process and you will enhance your odds for success.

Having a successful interview will significantly boost your chances of winning the job, although it's never guaranteed.

Many job hunters fail because they have no clue about the interview process and the employer's expectations. If you know what to say and do, you will have a successful interview.

Numerous banks, investment and legal businesses still adhere to professional dress codes and expect the same from their job candidates.

You will gain more bonus points by overdressing than underdressing. Always wear professional clothing or at least business casual clothing. Never ever wear just casual clothing to an interview.

You need to show you care, you've made a great deal of effort and you're interested in the position. The employer will be analysing whether you are a good fit for the company and that you will make a good representative for the company.

The way you carry yourself in a business environment will have a positive or negative effect on a successful interview. This is especially vital with the way you handle yourself in the presence of the interviewer.

One of the most important things to remember is to maintain eye contact with the interviewer. If you are looking around the room, out the window and not paying attention, the interviewer will end the interview and you will lose the opportunity to secure the job.

Some people are very good at interviewing techniques, while others do not have the faintest idea of what to do. If you're not working, or you'll be finishing up soon, or just frustrated with your current position interviewing can be incredibly stressful.

Being successful during the interview process goes beyond simply showing the interviewer you have the right qualifications for the job. In fact, being qualified for the job only guarantees you will be granted an interview.

It doesn't guarantee you will be hired for the job. **The key to being hired is selling yourself to the interviewer and that means you must go above and beyond demonstrating the extent of your skills.**

Millions of people apply to jobs they are not qualified to do on paper, men more so than woman. They try to convince the interviewer they have the skills to do the job. Even if you think you are the most coachable person in the world, **you should have the experience, or the ability to learn quickly.**

Several years ago, I had a friend who came across an opportunity to be a Web Designer for a well-known global organisation. He was used to building websites for small businesses using WordPress and helping them with their SEO.

The company had struggled for twelve months to find someone to fill this role. My friend got himself an interview.

The Hiring Manager and Director of the company asked him if he was able to develop websites using another coding platform that was less common in the industry. In the interview, he said he could do it, even though he had never used it before.

They asked him to develop a website for them in 4 days. He spent the few days he had for around 20 hours a day learning about the software, the coding language, the platform and developed the website.

To cut a long story short, ultimately, he was hired by the company and the position transitioned into being a Web Director. He built his own team who do all the required technical work. My friend was more of a salesperson than a technical guy.

I would love to tell you about more of his story (maybe in my next book) and how his role developed over time. He's a very charismatic man who believed in himself, sometimes you need to take a risk, but not everyone has the capability to do what he did.

TAKE A RISK AND STEP OUTSIDE YOUR COMFORT ZONE

Demonstrating to your potential employer you know something about the company, will also help increase your chances of being chosen for the role.

When you show you have enough interest in the company, take the time to learn about its history, products and services. You will gain brownie points in the mind of the interviewer.

The training process becomes much easier if you have done your research. It is very time-consuming explaining to someone who knows nothing about a company why they do specific things and what the company's mission, vision and values are.

Attitude is Everything

The way you carry yourself and the attitude you display to the interviewer will lead to interview success or failure.

You need to sell yourself during an interviewer, highlighting your skills, experience, education and abilities.

This should be displayed in a **confident manner with an attitude that gives the impression you believe your skills are by far greater than anyone else.**

You want to be confident and portray that you are the best person for the job, without being arrogant.

If you have negative feelings towards your current or previous employers, this should be kept to yourself.

Always talk positively about your experience, what knowledge you have acquired and strategies, processes and techniques you can implement in your next role.

That doesn't mean you lie about what happened but just do not dwell on the negatives and keep it short and sweet.

Never enter your interviewer's office with a 'Negative Nancy' or 'Debbie Downer' attitude (I apologise if your name is Nancy or Debbie - I don't mean you).

If you've had an argument with your partner, or another personal issue, leave those negative vibes at the door. The interviewer couldn't care less if you had a fight with your partner before the interview.

All they want to know is if you can do the job, fit into their team and add value to the company. Nobody likes being surrounded by people with negative energy as it affects everybody else's mood.

Don't get offended or pissed off if you discover that you must take a drug and alcohol test if you're successful for the job. The interviewer can pick up on your body language and tell if you have something to hide.

Action Verbs

Action verbs in your resume will help you get selected for a job interview. Hiring managers search by keywords to find resumes that match the job requirements they listed in the job description or job advertisement.

These power verbs can also help you to bring your interview to life. They paint a picture for the interviewer by highlighting your skills and accomplishments, support your communication skills and **help you stand out from the crowd.**

On the next page, there are some 'Action Verbs' to help you craft your interview answers to commonly asked interview questions (listed on page 41 to 51). **If you're not using these action verbs in your resume, you may be getting bypassed by the computer software that companies use.**

Action Verb Examples

Management

Administered	Analysed	Assigned	Authorised
Chaired	Collaborated	Co-ordinated	Delegated
Developed	Directed	Evaluated	Improved
Initiated	Integrated	Increased	Organised
Oversaw	Planned	Prioritised	Produced
Recommended			

Communication

Addressed	Arbitrated	Arranged	Authored
Communicated	Corresponded	Drafted	Edited
Enlisted	Formulated	Influenced	Interpreted
Listened	Mediated	Moderated	Negotiated
Persuaded	Promoted	Publicized	Directed
Lectured			

Research

Clarified	Codified	Collected	Contributed
Conducted	Critiqued	Examined	Extrapolated
Inspected	Interpreted	Interviewed	Evaluated
Investigated	Organized	Reviewed	Summarised
Surveyed	Systematised	Validated	Diagnosed
Tested			

Technical

Assembled	Built	Calculated	Computed
Converted	Customized	Engineered	Formatted
Maintained	Operated	Overhauled	Programmed
Simplified	Synthesized	Reconfigured	Remodelled
Repaired	Retrieved	Designed	Upgraded
Processed			

Teaching

Adapted	Advised	Clarified	Coached
Co-ordinated	Developed	Elaborated	Enabled
Encourage	Evaluated	Explained	Facilitated
Guided	Informed	Instructed	Mentored
Persuaded	Set Goals	Stimulated	Trained
Tutored			

Financial

Administered	Allocated	Analysed	Appraised
Audited	Balanced	Budgeted	Calculated
Estimated	Forecasted	Invested	Managed
Marketed	Negotiated	Reconciled	Reduced

Creative

Acted	Conceptualized	Created	Customized
Designed	Devised	Directed	Established
Fashioned	Founded	Illustrated	Initiated
Integrated	Performed	Revitalized	Visualised

Helping

Assisted	Assessed	Clarified	Coached
Counselled	Demonstrated	Diagnosed	Educated
Facilitated	Guided	Mentored	Motivated
Referred	Represented	Trained	Supported

Clerical

Approved	Arranged	Catalogued	Classified
Collected	Compiled	Dispatched	Distributed
Generated	Implemented	Inspected	Monitored
Operated	Organised	Reviewed	Scheduled

Accomplishments

Achieved	Adapted	Expanded	Established
Exceeded	Implemented	Improved	Led
Pioneered	Reduced	Resolved	Restored
Surpassed	Transformed	Won	

Adverbs

Accurately	Consistently	Convincingly	Continuously
Correctly	Creatively	Decisively	Directly
Easily	Effectively	Efficiently	Effortlessly
Frequently	Increasingly	Independently	Innovatively
Kindly	Meticulously	Methodically	Naturally
Patiently	Primarily	Positively	Proactively
Promptly	Purposefully	Routinely	Respectfully
Systematically	Skilfully	Strategically	Thoughtfully
Technically	Thoroughly	Passionately	Proficiently
Successfully	Strongly		

Commonly Asked Interview Questions

You need to demonstrate at an interview you are the right fit for the role, preparation is vital.

Use these common interview questions to prepare relevant responses matching your skills and traits to the needs of the company and role wherever possible.

Remember to also prepare compelling examples to help convince the interviewer you are the best person for the job.

Preparation, positivity and proof are your keys to interview success.

Q. Tell me about yourself?

- This is a commonly asked question designed to break the ice.
- Give a brief, concise description of who you are and your key strengths and skills.

Q. What do you know about our company?

- The interviewer really wants to assess your pre-interview preparation for the job.
- The interviewer is also testing to see if you are truly interested in the position.

Q. Why do you want to work here?

- The interviewer is trying to find out your enthusiasm for the role, as well as your level of knowledge about the company.

- Give specific examples of things that attracted you to the company and elaborate on them.

A Clever Guide To Winning The Job Interview

Q. What are your strengths?

- The interviewer wants to know what you are particularly good at.
- Choose a few of your key strengths required for the role and give examples.

Q. What is your greatest weakness?

- The interviewer is trying to test your self-awareness. We all have weaknesses, so it's best not to say you don't have any.

- Avoid using the word **'weakness'** and specify a 'challenge' that you are working to overcome.

Finish your answer with a positive, For example:

One of my biggest **challenges** is that I can't sit still and focus for long periods. I prefer hands-on activities.

To make sure that I got through school with good grades, I set study goals for myself.

I would sit still and focus on tasks for thirty minutes and take a short break.

After, I completed the activity I would reward myself.

This approach taught me discipline and helped me focus and I graduated from high school.

Q. What have been your achievements to date?

- The company is trying to establish how your accomplishments will benefit them.
- Select one or two accomplishments.
- Identify the situations, the actions you took and skills you used to get a positive outcome.

Q. What is the most difficult situation you have faced at work or school?

- The interviewer is trying to find out your definition of 'difficult'.
- They want to see if you can show a logical approach to problem solving.
- Select a tough situation that was not caused by you.

Q. What did you like & dislike about school/last job?

- The interviewer is trying to find out your key interests.
- They want to know whether the job on offer has responsibilities you will dislike.
- Focus on what you particularly enjoyed at school and what you learned from it.
- When addressing what you disliked, be conscious not to criticise too much.

Q. What are your goals for the future?

- A sense of purpose is an attractive feature in a candidate.

- This question probes your ambition and the extent of your career planning.

- Describe how your goal is to continue to grow, learn, develop and add value.

  Say you would like to work your way up in the company and become a leader. Businesses invest a lot of time and money in you. If they get the slightest hint, you won't be around for long. They will not hire you

Q. How do you respond to working under pressure?

- The interviewer wants to see you can stay focused in difficult conditions.

- Give an example of how you remained calm, in control and got the job done.

Q. Tell me about a successful team project you have been involved in. What was your role and what made it a success?

- The interviewer is trying to discover your interpersonal skills and team contribution.

Additional Interview Questions You Might Be Asked

- ✓ What makes you unique?
  _____
  _____
  _____
  _____
  _____

- ✓ What interests you about this role?
  _____
  _____
  _____
  _____
  _____

- ✓ What motivates you?
  _____
  _____
  _____
  _____
  _____

- ✓ What are you passionate about?
  _____
  _____
  _____
  _____
  _____

- ✓ Why are you leaving your current job?
  _____
  _____
  _____
  _____
  _____

- ✓ Where do you see yourself in five to ten years?
  _____
  _____
  _____
  _____
  _____

- ✓ What is your salary range expectation?
  _____
  _____
  _____
  _____
  _____

- ✓ How do you handle stress?
  _____
  _____
  _____
  _____
  _____

- ✓ What does customer service mean to you?

  _____
  _____
  _____
  _____
  _____

- ✓ What skills would you bring to the job?

  _____
  _____
  _____
  _____
  _____

- ✓ How do you define success?

  _____
  _____
  _____
  _____
  _____

- ✓ What is your dream job?

  _____
  _____
  _____
  _____
  _____

- What can you bring to the company?
  _____
  _____
  _____
  _____

- How do you handle conflict at work?
  _____
  _____
  _____
  _____
  _____

- Describe a time when your manager was wrong. How did you handle the situation?
  _____
  _____
  _____
  _____
  _____

- What makes you uncomfortable?
  _____
  _____
  _____
  _____
  _____

- ✓ How would you feel about reporting to a person younger than you?

  _____
  _____
  _____
  _____
  _____

- ✓ What is your ideal working environment?

  _____
  _____
  _____
  _____
  _____

- ✓ What differentiates you from our other candidates?

  _____
  _____
  _____
  _____
  _____

- ✓ Are you a morning person?

  _____
  _____
  _____
  _____
  _____

- ✓ Describe a time you went above and beyond at work?

- ✓ How would your friends describe you?

- ✓ Are you more of a leader or a follower?

- ✓ Do you have a personal mission statement?

- ✓ Tell me about the last mistake you made?

- ✓ What do you like most about yourself?

- ✓ Can you explain these gaps in your resume?

- ✓ Are you willing to travel?

- ✓ How long do you expect to work for this company?
  _____
  _____
  _____
  _____
  _____

- ✓ How do you keep yourself organised?
  _____
  _____
  _____
  _____
  _____

- ✓ What character traits would your friends use to describe you?
  _____
  _____
  _____
  _____
  _____

- ✓ What is your favourite movie of all time and why?
  _____
  _____
  _____
  _____
  _____

- ✓ What are three skills or traits you wish you had?
  _____
  _____
  _____
  _____
  _____

- ✓ Would you be willing to work nights and weekends?
  _____
  _____
  _____
  _____
  _____

- ✓ What qualities make a good leader?
  _____
  _____
  _____
  _____
  _____

- ✓ Describe your perfect company?
  _____
  _____
  _____
  _____
  _____

- ✓ What do you want to accomplish in the first thirty days of this job?
  _____
  _____
  _____
  _____
  _____

- ✓ Describe a time you got angry at work?
  _____
  _____
  _____
  _____
  _____

- ✓ Describe a time when you had to give a person difficult feedback?
  _____
  _____
  _____
  _____
  _____

- ✓ Do you prefer to work alone or on a team?
  _____
  _____
  _____
  _____
  _____

- ✓ How do you want to improve yourself in the upcoming year?

  _____
  _____
  _____
  _____
  _____

- ✓ What is the name of our Director?

  _____
  _____
  _____
  _____
  _____

- ✓ Who are your heroes?

  _____
  _____
  _____
  _____
  _____

- ✓ Would you ever lie for a company?

  _____
  _____
  _____
  _____
  _____

- ✓ What do you really think about your previous boss?

  _____
  _____
  _____
  _____
  _____

- ✓ What is your favourite memory from childhood?

  _____
  _____
  _____
  _____
  _____

- ✓ What is your favourite website?

  _____
  _____
  _____
  _____
  _____

- ✓ If you suddenly gained the ability to time travel, what's the first thing you'd do?

  _____
  _____
  _____
  _____
  _____

- ✓ When were you most satisfied in a previous job?
  _____
  _____
  _____
  _____
  _____

- ✓ What questions haven't I asked you?
  _____
  _____
  _____
  _____
  _____

- ✓ What's the last book you read?
  _____
  _____
  _____
  _____
  _____

- ✓ What is the best job you ever had?
  _____
  _____
  _____
  _____
  _____

- ✓ What is your greatest fear?

  _____
  _____
  _____
  _____

- ✓ What has been the most rewarding experience of your career/ life so far?

  _____
  _____
  _____
  _____

- ✓ What was your greatest failure, and what did you learn from it?

  _____
  _____
  _____
  _____

- ✓ Why are you changing careers?

  _____
  _____
  _____
  _____

- ✓ What's the biggest lesson you've learned from a mistake you've made?
  _____
  _____
  _____
  _____
  _____

- ✓ Can you walk us through your resume?
  _____
  _____
  _____
  _____
  _____

- ✓ How much do you expect to be earning in five years?
  _____
  _____
  _____
  _____
  _____

- ✓ What was the last project you led and what was the outcome?
  _____
  _____
  _____
  _____
  _____

- ✓ How would you deal with an angry customer?

  _____
  _____
  _____
  _____
  _____

- ✓ If you won $10 million on the lottery, would you still work?

  _____
  _____
  _____
  _____
  _____

- ✓ Which is more important, creativity or efficiency?

  _____
  _____
  _____
  _____
  _____

- ✓ Do you ever take your work home with you?

  _____
  _____
  _____
  _____
  _____

- ✓ Describe a time you chose to not help a teammate and why?

_____
_____
_____
_____
_____

- ✓ What three things are most important to you in your job?

_____
_____
_____
_____
_____

- ✓ What is one negative thing your last boss say about you?

_____
_____
_____
_____
_____

- ✓ What will you miss about your previous job?

_____
_____
_____
_____
_____

- ✓ Describe your work style?

- ✓ Who was your favourite manager and why?

- ✓ What is your management style?

- ✓ Who has affected you most in your career?

- ✓ Who are our competitors?

  _____
  _____
  _____
  _____
  _____

- ✓ Is it better to be good and on time or perfect and late with your work?

  _____
  _____
  _____
  _____
  _____

- ✓ Do you prefer working alone or in a team environment?

  _____
  _____
  _____
  _____
  _____

- ✓ Do you find it difficult to adapt to new situations?

  _____
  _____
  _____
  _____
  _____

- ✓ Do you have a mentor?

- ✓ What do you know about our industry?

- ✓ Explain why you've had so many jobs?

- ✓ What do you do in your spare time?

- ✓ What do you want to accomplish in the first ninety days of this job?
  _____
  _____
  _____
  _____
  _____

- ✓ Do you think you could have done better in your last job?
  _____
  _____
  _____
  _____
  _____

- ✓ Describe your top three technical skills?
  _____
  _____
  _____
  _____
  _____

- ✓ How would you fire someone?
  _____
  _____
  _____
  _____
  _____

✓ What causes are you passionate about?

Prepare Your Own Quality Questions

During an interview, it's always good to have some questions of your own ready to ask. Even though the interviewer may go through many topics of the job and company, and maybe even cover all your questions. Showing you have taken the time to prepare questions shows you have drive and initiative, both qualities that will help you secure the position.

Often, if you decline to ask any additional questions, the interviewer will see you as lacking any real initiative and you would fail the most important stage of the hiring process.

The questions you develop should be those that are out of the ordinary, not those that interviewers routinely answer. You can develop a different line of questions if you take the time to research the company before the interview. The information you find will never cover all the things you may want to know.

Pick out events from the company's history and ask questions that will provide the interviewer with a topic on which to expand.

Be careful when you choose your quality questions, you don't want to choose those that will stump the interviewer. **Choose less obvious questions, those that the company is more likely to make sure its employees know.**

Although you may ask questions about benefits if the interviewer doesn't cover them, do not ask about salary. Most people want to jump into this question quickly, but it makes the interviewer think that to you, the salary is more important than the job and it's a sure-fire way to lose the job before you have even got going.

If you have a minimum salary requirement, you can discuss that when the company makes an offer of employment. You also don't want to go too deeply into holidays, making it appear you are more interested in the benefits of the job rather than the position itself. You can get more specific when a job offer is made, and if you don't like the terms, you can negotiate or decline the company's offer.

The questions you want to ask are those directly related to the job and the company history, how it has evolved over the years, sales records, quality standards and the like.

Quality Questions To Ask The Interviewer

Before your interview, prepare questions you want to ask the interviewer.

'Open-ended' questions that begin with...

'What?'

'How?'

'Where?'

'When?'

'Who?'

should encourage your interviewer to talk and provide you with additional information.

Possible Questions Include:

- ✓ Can you give me more detail of what my role will involve?
- ✓ How has the position become available?
- ✓ How will you monitor/assess my performance?
- ✓ How many employees does the company have?
- ✓ How many people are in the team I will be working with?

- ✓ How long have you been with the company?
- ✓ What are the team dynamics/culture?
- ✓ Who will I report to, or who will be my supervisor?
- ✓ What projects has the company recently been working on?
- ✓ Do you have any other upcoming projects?
- ✓ What do you enjoy most about working here?
- ✓ Where is the company heading?
- ✓ What are the major issues facing the organisation or industry?
- ✓ What challenges do you think I will encounter in the first 30 to 60 days?
- ✓ How do you differentiate your business from your competitors?
- ✓ How do you manage or lead your team?
- ✓ What opportunities are there for career progression?
- ✓ What's involved in the training program?

First Impressions Count

The first impression is the last impression, and this is especially true of job interviews. If you cannot present yourself favourably at first glance, you will not have a second chance.

When you walk into the interview, you want to make the interviewer want to take a second look and create the impression you will be a valuable asset to the company.

Sometimes there may be allowances, such as when you work for a company with a casual dress code, and you are going for an interview immediately before or after work.

In this circumstance, you want to tell the interviewer of the situation so that it will not cast you in a negative light when you arrive.

Should You Ask About Pay?

There are many arguments for and against bringing up pay in an interview. I would strongly suggest not to mention pay unless the employer or hiring manager mentions it first. Then it is fair game to discuss the pay structure.

The reason I recommend this is because if this is your first gig, then pay even though it is very important should not even be on your radar. What I mean by this is that you should be thinking long term, along the lines of the skills, knowledge and experience you can acquire from the position which will be far more valuable than a few extra dollars now in your pay packet.

On the other side of the argument, I have friends and colleagues that say you should know your value and your worth. If we take a first-year apprenticeship wage in Australia.

Depending on the industry and the employer it could be a difference anywhere from $9 per hour up to $18 per hour. Therefore, based on a 40 hours week that is a difference of $360 per week.

Do your research and check out the Australian Apprentice & trainee pay rates:
https://www.fairwork.gov.au/pay/minimum-wages/apprentice-and-trainee-pay-rates

If you're adamant you want to bring up pay, be careful how you phrase the question. You could say something like "Is there an opportunity for overtime?"

The employer will be thinking that you're interested in working more hours than expected and it helps to open the conversation about wages, without directly asking.

Say what you feel is comfortable for you. My advice is to get the job and you'll be in a stronger negotiating position, as you know they want you for the position.

Closing Out The Interview

Scarcity and Urgency

Robert Cialdini published a book a book called *The Psychology of Persuasion* in 1984. One of the seven principles discuss scarcity. People are motivated by the thought that they might miss out on an opportunity. It's human nature to want what we can't have.

You can use this to your advantage to create urgency and scarcity. Towards the end of the interview, if it went well, the recruiter or hiring manager usually will ask what other job opportunities you have applied for, or what job interviews you have attended or have got lined-up.

I'm not telling you to say you have millions of job offers on the table, because that can backfire, and you will be left with nothing.

I've seen it happen to a few candidates in my recruitment days when negotiating salaries who have come back to me with their tail between their legs after trying to pull a fast one.

You want to portray that you are in high demand and a hot commodity who will not be in the job market for long. A great way is to say that you're waiting to hear back from a couple of interviews you've attended.

If they ask you for the details, you're not obliged to share, and you can say that you'd prefer not to share any details at this stage. If news gets out, there is always a danger that things can happen, and opportunities are sabotaged or withdrawn. I've heard of it happening many times before.

When I was a recruiter, hiring managers often passed on candidates simply because they felt like the jobseeker didn't really want the job. At the end of the interview, close by saying something like,

"Thank you for taking the time to meet with me today. I enjoyed learning more about (something specific). I am interested in the direction of (a particular) project. I look forward to continuing this conversation."

And if you know you want the job, say so. Don't leave any ambiguity. If you're excited about the opportunity and want to move forward with the company, say it.
People want to hire people that really want the job. Sometimes you do only get what you ask for.

Interview Hints & Tips

With the right preparation, you can answer key questions, sell your strengths and convince the interviewer you can add value to the company and that you are the right person for the job.

Research the company

- ✓ Researching the company shows initiative, enthusiasm and a keen interest in the role.

    - o Company websites and LinkedIn are the best sources of information.

    - o Use them to research products, services, projects and the interviewer's background.

- ✓ Research the person that will be interviewing you.

- ✓ Research other people in the company.

Research the role

- ✓ Think about the role and analyse the job details.

- ✓ Wherever possible, relate your skills and experience to the role requirements.

- ✓ Focus on the skills you believe offer the most value to your prospective employer.

- ✓ Always have practical examples ready to support your answers.

- ✓ Prepare your own quality questions.

- ✓ Remember that the interview is a two-way process.

Before the interview

- ✓ Make sure your social media is set to private, or delete any inappropriate material as employers search information about you and will judge you by what they see.

- ✓ Dress appropriately.

- ✓ Remember, you only get one chance to make a great first impression.

- ✓ It's better to overdress than to underdress.

- ✓ Take a common-sense approach and make sure that you know:
  - The time and location of your appointment.
  - The name and title of the person who will be interviewing you.
  - Write this information down and remember to use a GPS, or Apple/ Google maps.

- ✓ If you are going to be late, call ahead and let the interviewer know.

During the interview

- ✓ Have confidence in your research and preparation.

- ✓ Relax, listen carefully to the questions and keep your responses concise and positive.

- ✓ Use practical examples to illustrate your skills and show how they suit the role and the company.

- ✓ Maintain eye contact and remain attentive throughout.

After the interview

- ✓ Write down a short summary of the interview while it is still fresh in your mind.

- ✓ Note the areas in which you feel you went well, as well as any questions you found difficult to answer.

- ✓ This will help you to prepare for a possible second interview, work experience or with future interviews for other roles.

Self-Assessment Framework

Think about the whole interview from the time you showed up to the time you left

- ✓ How are you feeling about the whole experience?

- ✓ Who did you meet with?
    - o What did you think of them?

- ✓ How did they describe the opportunity to you?

- ✓ What did you like best about the interview?

- ✓ How did you describe yourself to the interviewer?

- ✓ How did they describe the role of someone who is successful in that position?

- ✓ How did you show them you would reach that level of success?

- ✓ Did you use specific examples of your past experiences?
    - o How did they respond to that?

- ✓ Did they discuss salary?
    - If so, who brought it up?
    - What did they say about it?
    - How did you respond?
    - What happened next?

- ✓ How do you think they perceived you based on your meeting?

- ✓ What are the concerns you think they have about you?
    - How did you handle those concerns?

- ✓ Based on the interview, how are you feeling about the opportunity now?

- ✓ What did you learn about the company that you didn't know before?

- ✓ Would you enjoy working there?

- ✓ Is there anything keeping you from moving forward to the next stage of the interview process?

- ✓ How did they leave everything?

- ✓ What did they say would happen next and when?

- ✓ Did you book another meeting right there and then?

- ✓ On a scale of 1-10 (10 being the highest) what would you rate your overall experience with the interview on how it went?
    - o If not a 10, what could you have done differently to have scored a 10/10?

- ✓ If they offered you the job, would you take it?
    - o If yes, how soon could you start?
    - o If no, why?

- ✓ Are there any concerns about the location of the position?

- ✓ Do you need to consult anybody else about your decision for this job opportunity?

- ✓ What other opportunities do you have pending right now?

Should I Say Yes To Accepting The Job Offer

I believe you should accept the job offer if you can say 'YES' to these 4 questions.

1. Are you happy with the company's products and services?

2. Are you happy with the company location and the amount of travel that is involved?

3. Are you comfortable with the base salary, commissions, bonuses, allowances, etc.?

4. Are you happy with the role, job responsibilities and career trajectory?

If you have said no to any of those questions, I would suggest not to proceed, or think about what things you would like to see change and then discuss it.

TAKE ACTION & PRACTICE PRACTICE PRACTICE

GOOD LUCK!!!

"PLAY THE GAME..."

- ✓ I BELIEVE IN YOU
- ✓ YOU HAVE THE POWER TO CONTROL YOUR OWN DESTINY
- ✓ BELIEVE IN YOURSELF
- ✓ IF YOU FEEL NERVOUS, GOOD, THAT MEANS YOU WANT THE JOB
- ✓ TODAY IS THE DAY THAT YOU GRAB THE BULL BY THE HORNS AND TAKE THE NEXT STEP UP IN YOUR CAREER
- ✓ YOU ARE CAPABLE OF INCREDIBLE THINGS
- ✓ YOUR JOURNEY IS ABOUT TO BEGIN

Social Media:

Website Name:
https://dremclaughlin.com/

Website Name:
https://theinterviewplaybook.com/

Website Name:
www.jobsearchqld.com

Instagram Handle:
https://www.instagram.com/jobsearchqld/

Insta Personal:
https://www.instagram.com/x_cite8/

Facebook Handle:
https://www.facebook.com/Job-Search-Qld-506215996784980/

Facebook:
https://www.facebook.com/drejobsearchqld/

LinkedIn:
https://www.linkedin.com/in/andre888/

LinkedIn:
https://www.linkedin.com/company/istrato/

Online Practice Interviews:
https://live.vcita.com/site/0mrgu95tbg3dyx1k

THANK YOU!!!

Copyright ©

All Rights Reserved Worldwide.

www.ingramcontent.com/pod-product-compliance
Lightning Source LLC
Chambersburg PA
CBHW050314010526
44107CB00055B/2236